AMERICAN INDIAN LIFE

The Chumash
The Past and Present of California's Seashell People

by Danielle Smith-Llera

Consultant:
Brett Barker, PhD
Associate Professor of History
University of Wisconsin–Marathon County

CAPSTONE PRESS
a capstone imprint

Fact Finders Books are published by Capstone Press,
1710 Roe Crest Drive, North Mankato, Minnesota 56003
www.mycapstone.com

Library of Congress Cataloging-in-Publication Data
Names: Smith-Llera, Danielle, 1971- author.
Title: The Chumash : the past and present of California's seashell people /
    by Danielle Smith-Llera.
Description: North Mankato, Minnesota : Capstone Press, 2016. | Series:
    Fact finders. American indian life | Includes bibliographical references
    and index. | Description based on print version record and CIP data
    provided by publisher; resource not viewed.
Summary: Explains Chumash history and highlights Chumash life in
    modern society.
Identifiers: LCCN 2015046718 (print) | LCCN 2015043527 (ebook) | ISBN
    978-1-5157-0237-5 (library binding) | ISBN 978-1-5157-0241-2 (pbk.) |
    ISBN 978-1-5157-0245-0 (ebook pdf)
Subjects: LCSH: Chumash Indians—History—Juvenile literature. |
    Chumash Indians—Social life and customs—Juvenile literature.
Classification: LCC E99.C815 (print) | LCC E99.C815 S64 2016 (ebook) |
    DDC 979.4004/9758—dc23
LC record available at http://lccn.loc.gov/2015046718

Editorial Credits
Alesha Halvorson, editor; Richard Korab, designer; Tracy Cummins and
Pam Mitsakos, media researchers; Tori Abraham, production specialist

Photo Credits
Alamy: Debra Behr, cover (bottom), Lisa Werner, 10; Capstone Press: 19;
Getty Images: Carlos Chavez, 22, Smith Collection/Gado, 23, Spencer
Weiner, 24, 25; iStockphoto: roc8jas, 6, Terry Wilson, cover (background);
Library of Congress: The Jon B. Lovelace Collection of California
Photographs in Carol M. Highsmith's America Project, 4-5; Native Stock
Pictures: Angel Wynn, cover (top), 1, 9, 21 Top, 26; Newscom: Mike Perry
Stock/Connection Worldwide, 28; North Wind Picture Archives: 12-13,
14-15, 16-17, Nancy Carter, 7; Shutterstock: Joseph Sohm, 4-5 Background,
welcomia, 29 background; Wikimedia: Daderot, 5 (bottom right), 11

Printed and bound in China.
009464F16

Table of Contents

Honoring Traditions 4

Chapter 1 **Seashell People** 6

Chapter 2 **Chumash Struggles** 12

Chapter 3 **Chumash Communities Today** . . 18

Chapter 4 **Protecting Traditions** 24

Timeline 29

Glossary 30

Read More 31

Internet Sites 31

**Critical Thinking Using
the Common Core** 32

Index 32

Honoring Traditions

Dolphins glide past a crew of men and women paddling across the Santa Barbara Channel. Redwood and driftwood planks are sealed with tar and curve to form a 20-foot-long (6-meter-long) canoe, known as a *tomol*. Chumash people today can ride modern boats across the 21 miles (34 kilometers) of water to Santa Cruz Island. But on special occasions they honor Chumash history by traveling as their **ancestors** once did.

Older tribe members appreciate that young people join them on the ocean journey. Chumash of all ages work to protect their community and the traditions they nearly lost 200 years ago.

ancestor: family member who lived a long time ago

A Lompoc, California, mural features Chumash spearing fish from a tomol.

BASKET WEAVING

The Chumash people were well known for their baskets. Other tribes—and later the Spanish—were eager to trade goods for their finely-woven baskets. The baskets were used for grinding nuts, trapping fish, cooking and storing food, holding belongings, and carrying babies.

Weavers twisted tan-colored grass and wove it into baskets. They also coiled and sewed it together. They dyed some grasses black with mud or soaked the grass in water with a piece of iron. They wove the grasses into stripes, zigzags, and geometric designs. Some baskets were woven so tightly they could hold water.

The last of the Chumash's most experienced weavers died around 1915. Some Chumash weavers today find inspiration in their ancestors' work. Chumash baskets in museum collections today help them learn traditional techniques. Weavers avoid new materials and use wild grasses and natural dyes.

Chapter 1

Seashell People

The Santa Ynez Mountains run parallel with the coastline near Santa Barbara, California.

For more than 10,000 years, most Chumash people lived along the Pacific coast between the present-day cities of Paso Robles and Malibu, California. Some groups lived on islands in the Santa Barbara Channel. Other groups lived in the mountains of what is now Santa Barbara County.

Mild winters made daily life comfortable for the Chumash. They did not need heavy clothing or thick-walled homes. Bundles of cattails and grasses arranged in layers formed the walls and roofs of their dome-shaped houses called 'aps.

The Chumash did not need to farm because the ocean and land provided food all year. Men carved hooks from shells and bone to catch many kinds of fish, including swordfish. They hunted sea otters and seals with nets, spears, and harpoons. With traps and bows and arrows, they hunted deer, ducks, and rabbits.

Chumash women gathered edible plants all year. They found seaweed on the shore. They collected acorns from oak trees to pound into mash or flour. They made teas and jellies from wild strawberries and cherries. They cooked stews outside.

a reconstructed Chumash 'ap in La Purísima Mission State Historic Park, California

Harvesting acorns
Acorns played an important role in Chumash history. California tribes harvested as much as 600,000 tons (544,300 metric tons) of acorns a year.

EDUCATION

Busy daily life was like school for Chumash children. Their teachers were their elders. Up to 50 family members lived together in an 'ap. Women taught girls to gather, cook, and store food. Men taught boys to hunt and fish. Elders also taught the children Chumash history and beliefs through stories.

GOVERNMENT

The Chumash formed regional alliances to keep peace between their villages. The villages sent representatives to meet as a group. This council selected a head chief, called a *paqwot*, to help end arguments over fishing and hunting grounds.

The Chumash were deeply loyal to their village and to their chief, called a *wot*. He or she was often the wealthiest member of the village. The chief controlled the storehouses filled with the village's food.

The wot did not look after the village alone. A council of relatives offered advice. The village religious leader, known as a shaman, was also an important figure. He or she planned ceremonies and cared for villagers' health with wild plants, songs, and stone charms.

Chumash children learned about their history and culture from storytellers.

TRADE

Chumash people often paddled tomols to visit each other's villages to trade. Chumash living near the ocean exchanged fish and sea lion meat for the deerskins and acorns of Chumash living inland. Beads made of carved shells were used as money. *Chumash* is said to mean "bead maker," "seashell people," or "moneymakers."

elder: older person whose experience makes him or her a leader
alliance: agreement between groups to work together
representative: someone who is chosen to act or speak for others
council: group of people elected to make decisions for a larger group

CAVE PAINTINGS

The Chumash people treasure cave paintings made by their ancestors. No one knows the meaning of the red, black, and white symbols anymore. Experts believe that shamans added to the paintings over the last 1,000 years. They mixed ground-up minerals and charcoal with animal fat or plant juices to make paint. With fingers or animal-tail brushes they painted on the cave walls.

Chumash today consider the caves so *sacred* that they keep all but one of their locations secret. One cave is open to the public. The Chumash Painted Cave State Historic Park is in the Santa Ynez Mountains, near Santa Barbara. A metal gate at the cave entrance allows visitors to look in but not get close to the paintings by Chumash ancestors.

ancient Chumash cave paintings near Santa Barbara

SPORTS

The Chumash took village games seriously. Each village had an open, flat area for competitions. In "hoop and pole," a player tried to throw a spear through the center of a rolling wooden ring. In the game "shinny," whole villages played against each other. Using hooked sticks, hundreds of players tried to hit a small wooden ball through goal posts.

sacred: holy

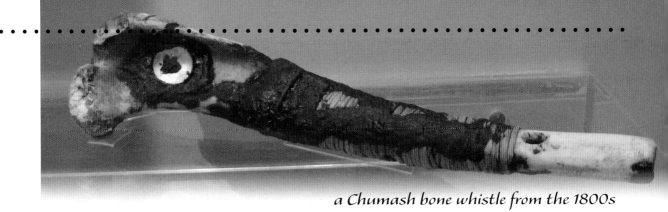

a Chumash bone whistle from the 1800s

CEREMONIES AND BELIEFS

Chumash villagers gathered to celebrate nature together. They wore California condor feathers and jewelry made of seeds, bones, stones, and shells. Chiefs and shamans often wore bearskin robes. They danced to the chirps of bone whistles and the beats of turtle rattles and wooden clappers.

In the fall they thanked the earth for the acorn harvest. During the winter they honored the sun and prayed for spring to come. They danced and wore masks to celebrate the animals and plants that fed their tribe.

SPANISH EXPLORERS

The Chumash tribe had grown to as many as 22,000 people by the 1500s. But their secluded village life was about to change. In 1542 Spanish ships sailed into the waters where only tomols had been paddled. The Chumash welcomed them with gifts.

Explorer Juan Rodriguez Cabrillo claimed Chumash land for Spain but left their villages undisturbed. For the next 200 years, Spanish ships stopped by the Santa Barbara Channel to prepare for long journeys across the Pacific Ocean. The Chumash continued living as ancient Chumash had for thousands of years.

Chapter 2

Chumash Struggles

Spanish missionaries built churches on Chumash land.

In the late 1700s, Russians explored the Pacific coast. Spain feared losing the Chumash lands Cabrillo had claimed. Spain sent Gaspar de Portolá to build forts on Chumash land in 1769. Spanish soldiers arrived to protect the settlements with guns and cannons.

Spain wanted to spread the Roman Catholic religion among the Chumash and other native peoples. Beginning in 1772 **missionaries** built churches and cleared fields for farming and raising cattle. The Spanish settlers often tried to lure the Chumash to the Catholic churches with goods, such as metal and cloth.

Spanish missionaries forced the Chumash to let go of their traditions. They took Chumash children away from their parents and brought them to live at the missions. Priests taught them about the Catholic religion. The children learned to speak Spanish. They wore wool clothing and learned to farm.

missionary: person who works on behalf of a religious group to spread the group's faith

Contact with the Spanish proved deadly for the Chumash. The Spanish carried diseases, such as measles and smallpox. Because of isolation from Europeans, the Chumash had no **immunity** to the diseases and thousands of tribe members died. Survivors of devastated villages were often forced to leave and find work at the missions.

Life at the missions was harsh for the Chumash. If they refused to work, the Spanish beat them or put them in jail. Their work with crops and cattle made the missionaries richer, but the Chumash often received no pay.

Mexico won independence from Spain in 1821 and took over the missions. But life for the Chumash did not improve. Mexican soldiers forced the unhappy Chumash to work long hours for no pay.

immunity: the ability of the body to resist a disease

In 1824 Mexican soldiers beat a Chumash boy at the Santa Ynez Mission. Angry Chumash set buildings on fire. News of the revolt sparked Chumash at other missions to fight. But when Mexican soldiers arrived with muskets and cannons, the Chumash put down their bows and arrows. Most returned to the missions.

The Chumash worked at California missions making baskets and rope.

By the late 1830s, only a few thousand Chumash were still living. The Chumash people and their traditions nearly became **extinct**. When Mexico lost the Mexican War in 1848, it gave up California to the United States. But U.S. laws did not protect Chumash land.

Thousands of Americans hurried west looking for gold after it was discovered in 1848. White settlers killed thousands of Chumash and other natives in the rush to take control of the land and the gold. More settlers moved west to set up farms and ranches when California became a state in 1850.

By the early 1900s, the Chumash had lost all of their land—except for one **reservation**, near the Santa Ynez Mission. But Chumash people today are proud to practice traditions their ancestors struggled to protect for hundreds of years.

extinct: no longer existing

reservation: area of land set aside by the government for American Indians; in Canada reservations are called reserves

Prospectors rushed to California in search of gold in the 1840s and 1850s.

17

Chapter 3

Chumash Communities Today

The Chumash once lived across 7,000 square miles (18,130 square kilometers) of present-day California. Today about 5,000 Chumash live on the Santa Ynez Reservation or in small communities along the coast.

Many Chumash **descendants** live in cities that once were missions, such as San Luis Obispo, Santa Barbara, and Ventura. Others live where their ancestors settled, in areas near Los Angeles and Bakersfield. Some Chumash share land with other California tribes.

Several Chumash groups hope the U.S. Congress will add them to the list of 566 federally recognized tribes. According to the Bureau of Indian Affairs, such tribes have a government-to-government relationship with the United States. This gives the tribes greater powers of self-government, federal aid, and a voice in federal Indian policy.

descendant: person who comes from a particular group of ancestors

The Santa Ynez Band of Chumash is the only federally recognized Chumash tribe. The U.S. government set up a 120-acre (48.5-hectare) reservation in present-day Santa Barbara County in 1901. Today less than one-fifth of the Chumash live on the reservation. But the Santa Ynez Reservation is growing. Its government bought an additional 1,400 acres (567 hectares) of land in 2010. Just a few families lived on the reservation in the 1930s. Today about 250 people live there, and new homes are under construction.

The Santa Ynez Reservation is located along the coast in southern California.

WORK

Chumash on the Santa Ynez Reservation are proud to live in an independent community, as their ancestors once did in villages. The Santa Ynez tribe has many businesses that earn money to care for its members and support nonprofit groups. Every day about 6,000 tourists visit the reservation. At the Chumash Casino Resort, they play bingo, cards, and other games, hoping to win money, just as their Chumash ancestors once placed bets on village games.

Tourists create jobs for the Santa Ynez Chumash. The reservation employs more than 1,700 Chumash in its hotel, restaurants, golf courses, casino, and gas station. The reservation provides shuttle services to take employees from three towns to and from work. It helps people pay for school. It also trains people for new jobs in order to help advance their careers.

Tourists and residents spend more than $200 million at Santa Ynez each year. The money helps pay for health care and educational and cultural programs for community members. The reservation also helps build roads and support schools and police departments outside the reservation.

traditional playing field at the Chumash Indian Museum in Thousand Oaks, California

TRIBAL COUNCILS

The Chumash admire how their ancestors ruled themselves in villages. The Coastal Band of the Chumash Nation, the Barbareño Chumash, and other Chumash communities elect their own chiefs and tribal councils.

The Santa Ynez Band of Chumash is proud of the **constitution** its members wrote in 1968. It created a **democratic** government led by the Business Committee. Every two years the community elects four members and a tribal chairman. The committee offers suggestions and community members vote.

constitution: legal document that describes the basic form of the government and the rights of citizens
democracy: form of government in which people elect their leaders

San Buenaventura Mission in Ventura, California

FERNANDO LIBRADO

Many Chumash traditions survive today because of the determination of Fernando Librado, also known as Kitsepawit. He was born around 1840 and was raised by his Chumash parents at San Buenaventura Mission, in present-day Ventura, California. His mother taught him the language of his island Chumash relatives and he also spoke the language of the Ventura Chumash.

Librado dedicated himself to protecting traditions before they were forgotten. While working as a shepherd, he traveled around the mountains near Lompoc, California, visiting Chumash homes. He listened closely to elders and learned their stories and songs.

He became friends with John Peabody Harrington in 1912. Harrington worked for the Smithsonian Institution, studying Chumash and other American Indian cultures. He wrote as many as 300,000 pages of notes based on what Librado and others told him. Librado died in 1915. But he left detailed information about Chumash history with Harrington.

Today Chumash are using Harrington's notes to rediscover their ancestors' dances, for example. The notes also preserve Librado's instructions for building a tomol. In 1976 a team built a tomol for the first time in more than 140 years.

Protecting Traditions

Chumash elders have always prepared young people to become responsible members of their village. Today the Santa Ynez Band of Chumash Education Committee provides lifelong learning programs.

Many Chumash children attend California public schools. But members of the Santa Ynez Band of Chumash Education Department work with teachers and parents to help Chumash students succeed in school. The education director helps Chumash students—and all of California's more than 6 million public school students—by serving on California's State Board of Education.

Students on the Santa Ynez Reservation study their native Chumash language.

The tribe hires tutors to come to the reservation's 5,000-square-foot (465-square-meter) education center. Chumash students get extra help with their schoolwork, if they need it. In the summer students from kindergarten through high school can work on math, reading, and science. The reservation makes it easier for tribe members to go to college. It pays for their courses and books—even their transportation and housing—while in school.

CHUMASH LANGUAGE

Ancient Chumash people never shared a common language. They spoke one of at least six languages in their villages scattered along the coast, on islands, and in the mountains. It is believed that more than 17,000 people spoke Chumash languages before the Spanish arrived.

The languages were nearly forgotten. In the missions Chumash children were forced to speak Spanish and forgot their ancestor's languages. Since the early 1900s, Chumash children have attended California public schools and learned English. The last Chumash person who spoke their ancestor's language died in the 1960s.

The Chumash are creating programs so that they can learn to speak their ancestors' languages again. They know how the languages sounded by using old recordings.

The notes of John Peabody Harrington help them pronounce Chumash words. He wrote them down using English letters.

Today the Santa Ynez Band of Chumash Indians has a weekly class for Chumash of all ages to learn their old languages. In 2007 they published a dictionary of 4,000 Chumash words translated into English.

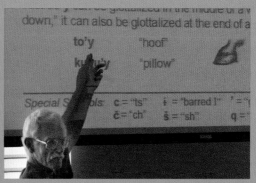

Richard Applegate, PhD, is a leading expert of the Chumash language and teaches Chumash natives at Santa Ynez's Tribal Hall.

HEALTHCARE

Santa Ynez tribe members combine new and traditional medicine to stay healthy. They visit doctors and dentists at the reservation's large, modern health clinic. If patients have low-paying jobs, the clinic charges them less for visits.

Doctors at the clinic sometimes recommend patients go to traditional healers. They use special plants as medicine. The clinic also runs traditional tribal "sweats," as their ancestors once did. They pour water over hot rocks in a special room and sit in the steam. Like their ancestors did, the clinic staff also takes special care of elders. The clinic organizes meals, crafts, and outings for them to share.

CONNECTION TO NATURE

Most Chumash today attend Catholic churches. But Chumash at Santa Ynez also remember their ancestor's beliefs to protect nature. Adults and children work together to care for the reservation's land and water. They plant and harvest zucchini, carrots, salad greens, and beets in a community garden on the reservation. They collect trash along the nearby beach.

The Santa Ynez Chumash Environmental Office checks for pollution in the Zanja de Cota Creek running through the reservation. Recycling bins encourage tribe members to recycle paper, plastic, cell phones, and batteries. They also recycle water by reusing it to cool buildings and water plants.

The Environmental Office works to keep air clean. Solar panels top the roofs of the Tribal Hall and Health Clinic. They can produce almost half of the electricity the buildings need. Some tribe members drive electric cars that do not pollute the air. They charge the car's battery instead of filling its tank with gasoline. Other drivers can fill their car tanks with specially prepared used cooking oil from the reservation's restaurants.

Reuse and recycle

Santa Ynez Chumash do not want trash from their annual powwow to go to landfills. They urge visitors to bring reusable water bottles and to throw trash into recycling bins. Special bins also collect unwanted food. The tribes feed it to animals.

CELEBRATIONS

The Chumash today still honor nature on the winter solstice in December—the shortest day of the year. They gather at various outdoor sites to celebrate the start of a new year. They remember their ancestors' foods by tossing acorn flour, chia seeds, and berries into fires. Storytellers and dancers perform for crowds of tribe members and visitors. The Chumash mark the site of the ceremony as their ancestors did. They dig a hole and place a tall, wooden pole into the ground. The pole is decorated with feathers.

For more than 50 years, the Chumash have hosted the Annual Inter-Tribal Powwow. Visitors from the United States and Canada travel to the Live Oak Campground on the Santa Ynez Reservation to celebrate Chumash and other American Indian traditions.

Drums beat as dancers compete for prizes. Artisans sell beaded

young dancers at the annual Santa Ynez Powwow

jewelry, leather bags, woven blankets, and animal furs. Chumash elders burn tobacco and the herb sage to bless visitors, as their ancestors would have. Chumash bring along their traditions as they move into the future.

TIMELINE

1542: Chumash meet Spanish ships lead by explorer Juan Rodriguez Cabrillo. He claims Chumash land for Spain.

1602: Spanish explorer Sebastian Vizcaino names Santa Barbara Bay.

1772: The Spanish build San Luis Obispo, the first mission on Chumash territory.

1804: The Spanish build Santa Ynez Mission, the last mission on Chumash territory.

1806: A deadly measles epidemic kills many Chumash.

1821: Mexico wins independence from Spain and takes over California.

1824: The Chumash revolt at Santa Ynez, La Purísima, and Santa Barbara missions.

1848: After winning a war against Mexico, the United States takes over California.

1849: Thousands of Americans rush west looking for newly discovered gold.

1901: The U.S. government establishes the Santa Ynez Reservation, the smallest in California.

1968: Members of the Santa Ynez Band of Chumash write their constitution.

1978: The Chumash protest against a utility company digging at an ancestral burial site at Little Cohu Bay. The protest lasts a year, and Chumash supervise all digging in the area.

2007: The Santa Ynez Band of Chumash publish a dictionary of Chumash words.

2009: President Barack Obama signs bill that includes text apologizing to American Indians for "many instances of violence, maltreatment, and neglect."

2012: An education center opens on the Santa Ynez Reservation.

2015: The U.S. Environmental Protection Agency recognizes the Santa Ynez for finding ways to reuse more than 13 tons (12 metric tons) of food waste rather than sending it to landfills.

GLOSSARY

alliance (uh-LY-uhns)—agreement between groups to work together

ancestor (AN-sess-tur)—family member who lived a long time ago

constitution (kahn-stuh-TOO-shuhn)—legal document that describes the basic form of the government and the rights of citizens

council (KOUN-suhl)—group of people elected to make decisions for a larger group

democracy (di-MAH-kruh-see)—form of government in which people elect their leaders

descendant (di-SEN-duhnt)—person who comes from a particular group of ancestors

elder (EL-dur)—older person whose experience makes him or her a leader

extinct (ik-STINGKT)—no longer existing

immunity (i-MYOON-uh-tee)—the ability of the body to resist a disease

missionary (MISH-uh-ner-ee)—person who works on behalf of a religious group to spread the group's faith

representative (rep-ri-ZEN-tuh-tiv)—someone who is chosen to act or speak for others

reservation (rez-er-VAY-shuhn)—area of land set aside by the government for American Indians; in Canada reservations are called reserves

sacred (SAY-krid)—holy

READ MORE

Chambers, Catherine. *American Indian Myths and Legends.* All About Myths. Chicago: Raintree, 2013.

Lowery, Linda. *Native Peoples of California.* North American Indian Nations. Minneapolis: Lerner Publications, 2015.

Sonneborn, Liz. *California Indians.* First Nations of North America. Chicago: Heinemann Library, 2012.

INTERNET SITES

FactHound offers a safe, fun way to find Internet sites related to this book. All of the sites on FactHound have been researched by our staff.

Here's all you do:

Visit *www.facthound.com*

Type in this code: 9781515702375

 Check out projects, games and lots more at **www.capstonekids.com**

CRITICAL THINKING USING THE COMMON CORE

1. How did the coming of the Spanish change Chumash lives? What impact did missions have on the Chumash after 1772? Would you say these changes did more harm or good? Why? (Integration of Knowledge and Ideas)

2. What do you think is the most important reason Chumash culture survives today? (Integration of Knowledge and Ideas)

3. In what ways does the ocean still influence Chumash today? (Key Ideas and Details)

INDEX

ancestors, 4–5, 10,16, 18, 20, 22–23, 25, 26–27, 28

bands, 19, 22, 24–25
baskets, 5
beliefs, 8, 11, 27

California, 6–7, 11, 16, 18–19, 22–23, 24–25
cave paintings, 10
ceremonies, 8, 11, 28
Chumash Casino Resort, 20
clothing, 6, 11, 13
communities, 4, 18, 20, 22, 27
councils, 8, 22
crafts, 9, 11, 26, 28

diseases, 14

education, 8, 20, 24–25
elders, 8, 23, 24, 26, 28

food, 5, 7, 8–9, 11, 27, 28

government, 8, 18–19, 22

Harrington, John Peabody, 23, 25
health, 8, 20, 26
history, 4, 8, 22–23
houses, 6, 8, 22

language, 23, 25
Librado, Fernando, 23

Mexico, 14–15, 16
missionaries, 13, 14–15
missions, 16, 18, 23, 25

nature, 11, 27, 28

paqwot, 8
population, 11, 18–19
powwows, 27, 28

reservations, 16, 18–19, 20, 25, 26–27, 28

Santa Ynez, 10, 15, 16, 18–19, 20, 24–25, 26–27, 28

Spain, 11, 13, 14
sports, 10, 20

tomols, 4, 9

villages, 8–9, 10–11, 20

work, 13, 14, 20